APPLIQUE
Lace
PATTERNS

Linda Pool

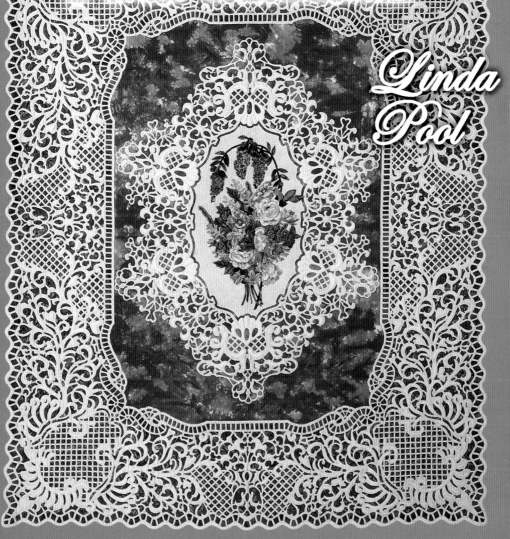

American Quilter's Society
P. O. Box 3290 • Paducah, KY 42002-3290
www.AmericanQuilter.com

Located in Paducah, Kentucky, the American Quilter's Society (AQS) is dedicated to promoting the accomplishments of today's quilters. Through its publications and events, AQS strives to honor today's quiltmakers and their work and to inspire future creativity and innovation in quiltmaking.

EDITOR: BARBARA SMITH
GRAPHIC DESIGN: ELAINE WILSON
COVER DESIGN: MICHAEL BUCKINGHAM
PHOTOGRAPHY: CHARLES R. LYNCH

Library of Congress Cataloging-in-Publication Data
Pool, Linda.
    Appliqué lace patterns / by Linda Pool.
       p. cm.
    Summary: "Three dozen appliqué patterns using a portable technique. Author provides tips on where to find design ideas and how to create a lacy appliqué pattern"--Provided by publisher.
    Includes bibliographical references.
    ISBN 1-57432-908-1
    1. Appliqué--Patterns.   2. Quilting--Patterns.   I. Title.
    TT779.P656 2006
    746.44'5--dc22

                                      2006008812

Additional copies of this book may be ordered from the American Quilter's Society, PO Box 3290, Paducah, KY 42002-3290; 800-626-5420 (orders only please); or online at www.AmericanQuilter.com. For all other inquiries, call 270-898-7903.

Proudly printed and bound in the United States of America

Dedication

This book is dedicated to my Lancaster County, Pennsylvania, Mennonite grandmother, Mary Groff Leaman. Her love of quilting, during seventy years of her life, inspired me to walk where she walked and explore this vast and endless world of ideas and creative outlets that is quilting. Even though she is gone, her love of quilting goes on through her daughters, Miriam Segerstrom, of Tucson, Arizona, and Irene Shenk, of Mt. Joy, Pennsylvania, who have both shared quilting with me and helped inspire me to continue this rewarding family tradition.

Contents

LACY SAMPLER, 92" x 108", by Sarah E. Luther, Fort Worth, Texas. Patterns
can be combined to make a bed-sized quilt.

Acknowledgments

With thanks ...

To my daughter Stephanie Pool, who lives so far away in California. She has always encouraged me to write a book. She has been an inspiration to me in more ways than she can know, especially since she began cutwork appliqué and started translating her stained-glass paintings into fabric. She gave me the biggest compliment she could by learning a technique from me and making it her own.

To my daughter Genelle, who, at the age of 17, was willing to try the cutwork technique. She has provided me with a sample to show other quilters who may be too timid to think they are able to tackle this wonderful, freeing, method of appliqué.

To my daughter-in-law, Amy, for showing her confidence in me by allowing me to teach her to quilt, first of all, and then to stitch a wonderfully creative cutwork project for her mother. Thank you to Amy and my son Chris, for making me a grandmother and giving me a granddaughter and two grandsons who appreciate fabrics and color.

To my sons, Chris and Kevin, and my husband, Don, for keeping my computer up and running and for helping me work out the mechanics of computing in all forms. I need you all and I love you all, dearly.

To my niece, Christy Leaman, for sharing her love of crafting with me and now cutwork appliqué as well.

To my best friend and walking companion, Barb Celio, who continually gives me support, guidance, and encouragement with her belief in me. Thank you for reading my written words and offering your editorial suggestions, for making samples for the book, and for being an all-around good sounding board for ideas, from child rearing to paint colors.

To my very good friend Colleen Buchanan, who is a prolific quilter as well as a wonderful "ideas person" when I'm in need of an inspiration.

To Hazel Carter, quilt historian, founder of the Continental Quilting Congress and the Quilters Hall of Fame, thank you for your confidence in me and my ability to create "something totally my own." You have been a great inspiration to me and a confidence booster.

Thanks to all the wonderful ladies who helped me sew the pattern blocks for this book.

To my dear friends and quilting students who have been begging me for years to write a book. Hope you will find this one a special tool as you continue to grow and develop your quilting skills.

And last, but by no means least, to my friends Hal Woodward and Debbie Stone for praying for me to have the courage to tackle this book. Your prayers were answered, and I benefited from them immensely.

Foreword

I have admired Linda Pool's work for many years. She has a special creative talent for adapting other media to quilt design. I first saw LINDA'S LACE when Linda was appliquéing the lace edges. It was gorgeous! I was so impressed with the lace doily translated into a quilt that I could hardly sleep that night.

One of the wonderful things about appliqué is that there are many different ways to do it. I love to try different techniques for my designs but prefer to use freezer paper and traditional appliqué techniques. I don't usually use reverse appliqué, but then Linda taught a lace class at my local quilt shop. I decided to take it because I love the idea of creating lace with appliqué and wanted to try Linda's techniques, the ones I usually avoid.

Linda's class was delightful. She brought her quilts to inspire us and encouraged us to design our own lace pieces. She gave us a sequence for stitching each part of the design and took us through the steps slowly. She gave us hints for making the appliqué easier, along with ways to mark and trim the fabric and use the needle to control curved edges. She changed my view of reverse appliqué and opened my eyes.

I am thrilled that Linda has written this book so that she can share her lovely designs and successful techniques with other quilters, and I am honored that she asked me to write the foreword. May you enjoy her designs and techniques as much as I do.

Mimi Dietrich

Made by Mimi Dietrich

LINDA'S LACE, 62" x 77", designed and sewn by the author. My love for lace inspired me to create a whole new look in quilting, starting with this quilt, which was nominated as "One of the Best Quilts of the Twentieth Century."

Introduction

Welcome beginners! The beginner and the experienced quilter alike can enjoy lacy appliqué. My daughter Genelle was helping me vend at a quilt show when she was 17 years old. She had never appliquéd before, but she kept listening to me tell other quilters how to do this technique. After a while she said, "Mom, let me try one of those kits." I gave her one, and she started working on it right away. She was very successful, even with no hand-stitching skills. I use her sample to show other quilters that, even with no experience, they too can have success with lacy appliqué.

Christy Leaman at 13

At 13 years old, my niece, Christy Leaman, wanted me to teach her the technique. I marked a design on fabric and showed her how to cut and stitch it. At 16, she still enjoys lacy appliqué.

My 27-year-old cousin, Dan Breneman, who was working with the Peace Corps in the backcountry of El Salvador, wanted a project to take back for the women's group he had started. I collected fabric, needles, thread, scissors, pins, and some of my patterns for him. I demonstrated lacy appliqué then asked him to try it. (He had only been taught to sew buttons on, by his mother.) He did an excellent job of the stitches he put into the block.

When Dan returned to El Salvador, he shared the technique with the village ladies. There were sixteen women ranging in age from 21 to 60. A week later, all the women had finished the project. Two women became very interested in the technique, and in a few weeks' time, they had made several tablecloths and pillowcases (butterfly pillowcase shown on page 12) from the patterns and fabrics I had sent. The women raffled the items to purchase a communal sewing machine.

In these pages, you will find many lacy appliqué patterns in different styles for you to trace or copy. You can use the patterns at the size presented or enlarge them as needed for your projects. If you prefer to create your own designs, I have also provided all the information you will need to find design ideas, represent them in a drawing on paper, and adapt them to make a lacy appliqué pattern.

If you have never done needle-turn appliqué before, start with a simple pattern, such as the Butterfly (pages 60-61) or the Picture Frame (page 92). Follow the instructions for Preparing to Appliqué (page 23) and The Appliqué Stitch (page 28).

Because lacy appliqué represents lace, you can relax with it. When have you ever seen a piece of lace in which all the cutout sections are exactly the same size and shape? It would be a rare piece of lace, indeed.

LEFT: Imperfections in lace do not detract from its beauty.

PILLOWCASE by 23-year-old Rosa Julia Rodriguez Cordova of El Salvador

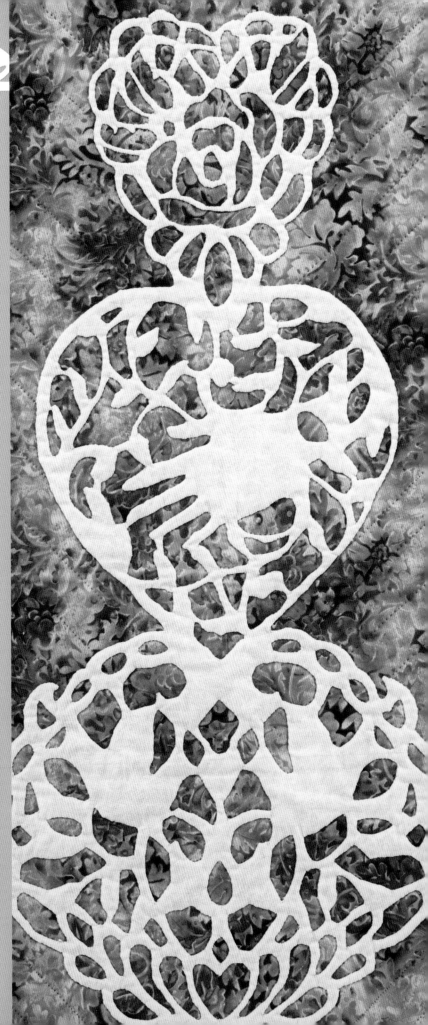

What is Lacy Applique?

Lacy appliqué is simple and fun to do. It requires few tools, and it's convenient to sew in spare moments and to take with you when you travel. Once you have selected a pattern from pages 55–109, you can choose to make it in one of three ways: negative-image design, positive-image design, or negative and positive combined.

RIGHT: MOTHER OF MY HEART, DETAIL, 15¼" x 29", stitched by Amy L. Pool, Haymarket, Virginia

Example of a negative-image design with multiple bottom fabrics. Notice that the top fabric becomes the block background (Lacy Flower Basket pattern on pages 78–79).

Negative-Image Design

If the cutout shapes draw your eye and form the pattern, the design is a negative image. In its simplest form, two fabrics are layered together, both right side up. Shapes are then cut out of the top fabric so the bottom fabric shows through, forming the design. The top layer is the positive image, and the bottom layer is the negative image. After basting and appliquéing the two layers together, trim the block to size for your project.

If you like, you can use multiple bottom fabrics for the negative shapes. To do this, place a bottom fabric under a shape or several shapes then baste and appliqué them. Cut away the excess bottom fabric from around each sewn shape. Repeat the process for the next bottom fabric and the next until all the shapes have been appliquéd. Then cut the block to size.

"You can take it anywhere and work on it anytime. I love it! You can do appliqué for a few minutes, or you can do it for hours."

JoAnn L. Capraro, Holiday, Florida

HEART #16, HAND IN HEART. This is an example of a positive-image design with a single bottom fabric. The bottom fabric becomes the block background (pattern available on author's Web site, provided on page 111).

Positive-Image Design

If your eye is drawn to the top fabric, the design is a positive image. The bottom fabric layer is an invaluable part of your design, however, because it is the background on which the positive image is displayed. In a positive-image design, the cutout shapes and the outside edge of the design are appliquéd to the bottom fabric.

Negative & Positive Combined

The Hearts and Feathers Lace Frame is a negative-image design because the negative shapes are prominent in the overall design. However, the whole piece could become a positive-image design if it is appliquéd to another fabric.

As an example of a combined image, the Lacy Flower Basket starts as a negative image, but it becomes a positive image when the whole piece is appliquéd to a new background fabric.

> **TIP.** Be sure to cut the background fabric at least 1" larger all around than the size of the finished block to allow for fraying during the appliqué process. Any frayed edges will then be cut off when the block is squared and cut to size.

HEARTS AND FEATHERS LACE FRAME, 31" x 39", designed and stitched by the author

On a third fabric, the Lacy Flower Basket becomes a positive image (pattern on pages 78–79).

For Quilters on the Go

Can't wait to get your hands on your sewing project? Lacy appliqué is very portable. Because it can be done with only two pieces of fabric, there are no small pieces to get lost. After a project is prepared for stitching, it can be carried in your purse, to pull out and work on in even the smallest time slots: during your coffee-break, waiting at a doctor's appointment, or anywhere you choose to sit down and relax for a few minutes. You'll be surprised at how quickly a project can be completed in just a few stitches at a time.

I have ladies who regularly send for patterns because they are going on vacation and want a project to work on while away from home. The supplies needed for this type of sewing project are minimal and easy to transport.

Lacy appliqué is also good for scissor-less airline travel. Because your block will be securely basted, you can precut as many shapes as you need for your flight. Clip the curves and points on each shape and put your scissors in the suitcase that you will be checking. That way, you will have the scissors when you arrive at your destination and can use them to cut sections for your return trip. Carry along a small thread cutter or a fingernail clipper for cutting threads during the flight.

LEFT: Tulips and Lace, 33" x 41", stitched by Inge Vogler, Cape Coral, Florida

Choosing Fabrics

Here are some suggestions for selecting fabrics for your project. This is an important step that can determine how much you enjoy the needle-turn process.

Top Fabric

The top layer needs to be a high-thread-count, 100 percent cotton that is easy to needle. If you want your finished piece to look more like lace, you may want to use a white or cream fabric on top because that's the usual color of lace. I prefer using white-on-white fabric with a small overall design, because the raised surface texture seems to help keep the fabric from fraying. The design in the white-on-white fabric also adds a lacy look to the positive image. Some of these fabrics are thin and loosely woven, so be careful when choosing them. It wouldn't hurt to sew a test piece before you mark the whole pattern on the fabric.

> **TIP.** A light-colored fabric is easier to sew than a dark one, because light colors are easier on the eye, and less light is required. If you have trouble seeing clearly, be sure to sew with a bright light over your left shoulder, if you are right-handed.

I have had success using light-colored batiks as the top fabric, also. They are nearly as easy to stitch as the white-on-white fabrics, and they have a high thread-count. Other fabrics can be used for lacy appliqué, including synthetics that don't fray, but I suggest that you have some experience before you try them.

Bottom Fabric

It would be best for the bottom fabric to be 100 percent cotton that is easy to needle, but it can be any fabric you want. The color can be anything at all. If you want the positive image to stand out in your block or quilt design, keep the bottom fabric pattern relatively simple. A two- or three-color pattern that looks like a solid when you squint your eyes should work well, even if it is a floral print.

If you use a busy, multicolored print for the background fabric, the positive image will appear to "bleed" into the background at places where the background pattern and the top fabric are similar in color. This effect will cause you to lose the distinct, crisp edges of the design. Try to use a bottom fabric that is totally different from the top fabric.

This positive-image Calico Cat is camouflaged when stitched on a busy background fabric.

The Calico Cat is now the center of attention on this bottom fabric (pattern on page 58).

Tuberose and Hoya appliqué block

There is no need to use just two fabrics for a positive-image design. You can use as many fabrics behind your pattern as you like in the negative shapes. With a little planning, your designs can be full of color and detail, and the creative options for lacy appliqué are endless.

Block Background

Let your fabric work for you. Background fabrics can make exciting additions to your design. Many of the fabrics on the market are printed with geometric or other lacy-looking images that can be used to enhance the appearance of lace. Using these fabrics in the negative spaces of your design can add a whole new dimension to your project.

To add to the lacy appearance of your piece, coordinate the color of the

Top fabric: white to match bottom fabric print
Bottom fabric: white lacy print on fuchsia
Block background: fuchsia to match bottom fabric

Black lace on yellow background

top fabric to the bottom fabric's lacy or geo-metric design. Then, for the block back-ground, choose a fabric to match the color of the bottom fabric's background. Even though three fabrics are used, it will look like only two, but the effect will be see-through lace.

Look closely at my lace frame, Hearts and Feathers Lace Frame. I used a piece of black-and-white fabric with a "torn-cheese-cloth" print for the negative spaces. When the completed piece was stitched onto a black background, the white of the positive image and the white cheesecloth became one. My quilt has caused many curious com-ments about the holes in the piece. The fab-ric really does fool the eye. To me it represents my love for old linens and lace.

HEARTS AND FEATHERS LACE FRAME (close-up), stitched by the author. The bottom fabric is a black-and-white print representing torn cheesecloth. Pat-tern available on author's Web site (see page 111).

HEARTS FOR DANNY AND JESSICA, 57½" x 67½", stitched by Jennifer Bisk, Reston, Virginia. A quilt made of all hearts would make a wonderful wedding present.

Preparing to Appliqué

For ease in handling, trace the pattern from the book onto tracing paper, or photocopy it, to make a master pattern. With photocopying, you have the advantage that you can easily enlarge the pattern if desired. To transfer the master pattern to the top fabric, there are several different methods you can use.

Direct Tracing

If you are marking the pattern on a light-colored fabric, you may be able to see through the fabric to the master pattern underneath. If so, you can trace the design without using any light source, as follows: Place the master pattern on a light-colored surface. A piece of white paper will work fine. Lay the fabric on top and, using a #2 sharp pencil, lightly trace the solid pattern lines.

If a darker fabric is used for the top, you may need to tape the master pattern and fabric to a window to do the tracing. If you have a light box, this would, of course, be preferable. No light box? Do you have a glass-topped table? Take the shade off of a lamp, set the lamp under the table, and use this set-up as a light box.

Making Stencils

If you want to make a stencil for marking your fabric, make a copy of the pattern. Use a small utility knife with a razor-sharp edge or small, sharp scissors to cut out the shapes. Be sure to cut away the lines, so that when you trace them on fabric, the shapes will be accurate. If using a utility knife, be careful because this is a very sharp tool, and you will need to do your cutting on a pad of newspapers or a rotary-cutting mat.

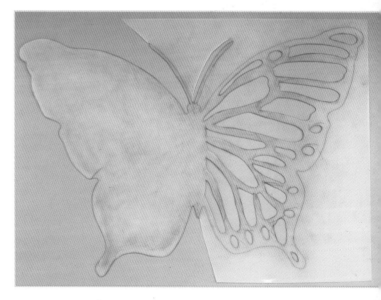

This stencil has been cut to retain its strength for tracing. Use one side of the stencil to trace the inner wing shapes and the other side to trace the antenna and wing outlines. Flip the pattern over to complete the other half of the butterfly.

Freezer-paper stencil pressed on fabric

To transfer the pattern to fabric, trace along the stencil with a #2 pencil for a light-colored fabric and use a white or silver quilter's pencil for a dark one. If you plan to use a pattern several times, you may want to trace it on template plastic and cut the shapes out with a small utility knife. You will then have a permanent stencil of the pattern.

Using Freezer Paper

Freezer paper can also be used to make a stencil. Lay the master pattern on a flat surface. Place a piece of freezer paper, dull side up, on top of the pattern and trace the lines. Cut the shapes with a small utility knife or scissors then discard the shapes. Iron the stencil on the top fabric, right side up. Trace around the stencil with a pencil, then remove the stencil. The freezer paper can be re-ironed, so it can be used again for another project.

I do not recommend leaving the freezer-paper stencil on the fabric while you are stitching. The paper gets in the way, and it makes the piece more difficult to handle.

Preparing the Fabric Layers

There are several steps in preparing the fabric layers for appliqué. These are simple to do and not time-consuming.

LEFT: MY ROMANTIC HEART, 12" x 14½", stitched by Jean Tate, Alamo, Texas

SLASH YOUR FABRIC

Yes, I did say "slash your fabric." You need to make a tiny slit in each negative shape before you layer the top and bottom fabrics. This step will save you from having to tediously pick your fabric layers apart to begin cutting the negative shapes. It will also keep your scissors from accidentally piercing the bottom fabric.

To make the slashes, fold each shape in half and use a small, sharp scissors to make a small cut in the middle of the shape. If you prefer, you can lay the top fabric on a padding of newspapers and use a utility blade to make the slashes. Be sure to make all the slashes away from the edges of the shapes because you will need to leave a turn-under allowance.

BASTING THE LAYERS

Single bottom fabric. Center the top fabric over the bottom fabric and pin it in place. Baste the layers ⅛" to ¼" outside the marked line around each negative shape in the design. Also baste ¼" inside the edge of the block.

Thread basting is preferable to using straight pins, safety pins, or a basting gun. You will be much happier if you don't have sharp things to jab and poke at your hands as you work, or things that stick out and catch hold of the thread at every stitch.

Basting is an important step, so don't skimp on the stitching. Your layers will lie flatter and have fewer puckers from all the prodding, poking, and handling if they are basted thoroughly. Once the basting is finished and the pins removed, your project is ready to travel with you wherever you go.

Multiple bottom fabrics. Place the desired fabrics under the shapes to be cut out. The bottom fabrics can be changed with every shape, if desired. Make sure the weaves of the top and bottom fabrics run in the same direction to help keep the fabrics from buckling or warping in the negative shapes. If the fabric changes are close together, you will need to appliqué one fabric at a time.

When you have completed appliquéing the shapes, turn the block over to the wrong side and cut away the bottom fabrics ³⁄₁₆" from the stitching around each shape.

Appliqué with multiple bottom fabrics

Stitching Lacy Appliqué

Once the top and bottom fabrics have been basted, you are ready to start sewing. Because lacy appliqué is done by hand, you need only a few sewing supplies.

Sewing supplies

Appliqué Supplies

Scissors. It is really important to have sharp scissors for lacy appliqué. It doesn't matter what brand you use or what style, but the scissors need to be able to make small, clean clips with one motion. It should be able to cut sharp to its point and not get caught in the fabric at the point. Small 3" to 4" embroidery scissors are a good choice. You can even use the lipped appliqué scissors, if the points cut sharp. It would be a good idea to test your scissors on fabric before purchasing them.

Needles. The needles I recommend are #9 or #10 sharps. Try to use a needle with a small eye so that it doesn't make visible holes in the fabric's appliquéd edge. I am frequently told that people use straw needles for their needle-turn appliqué. I have tried them and found them unsatisfactory. In fact, I have tried several kinds at different times, but I bend the straw needle within 30 seconds of working with it. A bent needle just gets in the way.

Thread. I recommend a very fine thread. You will be putting a lot of stitches into this appliqué, so even if you use a thread with fewer plies than normal, the piece will still be securely sewn. My favorite is machine embroidery thread. This two-ply, 60-wt.100 percent cotton thread is sold in many colors.

Thimble. It is not necessary to use a thimble for appliqué if you are using fabrics that are easy to needle. However, some people prefer to protect their fingers while stitching. I can sew for hours and even days without needing a thimble and then, oops, the needle finally wears through my skin and starts to hurt. Then I put on a thimble! Now you are ready to begin cutting, sewing, and watching the design develop in front of your eyes. This is the rewarding part!

Preparing a Shape for Stitching

There are no raw edges to fray in your design because you cut the shapes out when you are ready to stitch them. To prepare a negative shape for needle-turn appliqué, slip the point of the scissors into the slash. You might want to start with one of the larger shapes in the design. Cut away the excess fabric inside the shape, leaving a ⅛" to ³⁄₁₆" turn-under allowance.

The only way to get the fabric to turn under smoothly without puckering is to clip the curves. Clip all outside curves every ⅛", staying just inside the pencil line. Your scissors should be sharp enough to make the whole cut with one snip. If you have to hack at the fabric, get a new pair of scissors.

On an outside point, clip just through the pencil mark so the mark will not show when the fabric is turned under. There will be little fabric to turn at this point. Do not mess around with this fabric because you do not want what little there is to fray. Secure any loose threads as you sew by taking a couple of stitches over the outside point.

Do not clip the inside curves or points. If the fabric is not turning under smoothly on an inside curve, stick your needle under the folded edge, catch the fabric with the point of the needle, and move it whichever direction it needs to go to smooth the edge. Make the fabric do what you want it to do!

Knotting the Thread

Finger-wrap knot. Cut a piece of thread 18" to 24" long. Thread the needle. Hold the thread in one hand about 2" from the end and, with your other hand, make the knot, as follows: Take the end of the thread between your thumb and index finger. Wrap the thread around your index finger and, with your thumb, roll the thread between the two fingers. Now, take this "roll" between a fingernail and your thumb and pull it to the end. This will leave a knot at the end of your thread.

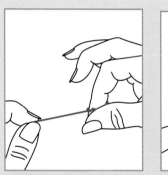

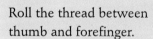

Roll the thread between thumb and forefinger.

Pull the "roll" to the end of the thread.

TIP. Notice that, for reverse appliqué, the terms "outside" and "inside" in reference to the curves and points are the opposite of conventional appliqué. Think of being inside the negative shapes.

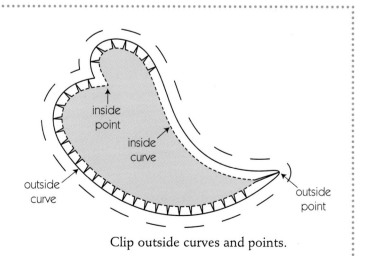

Clip outside curves and points.

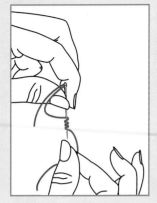

Wrap the end of the thread around the tip of the needle.

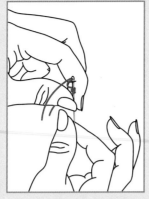

Pull the thread wraps off the eye end of the needle.

The Appliqué Stitch

The following instructions are for right-handed sewers. If you are left-handed, refer to the figures for your hand and needle positions.

Start sewing at an outside point. Hold the fabric in your left hand, with the edge you are about to sew on the side toward your lap, as shown in the figures. Have the fabric cradled between your thumb and first finger, with the first finger resting under the appliqué. Keep your thumb close to the edge you will be sewing so that it can hold the allowance in place as you turn it under with the needle.

Turn a small portion of the edge. Use the tip of your needle to grab the fabric edge and turn it under. As your left thumb catches the edge and holds it in place, slide the side of your needle down and to the right, smoothly turning under the edge for a distance of about ¾". This may take a little practice. It works best when your needle is held almost flat against the fabric as you slide it down.

Needle-wrap knot. Thread the needle. Holding the needle between your thumb and index finger, wrap the other end of the thread several times around the point of the needle, about half way down the length of the needle. With the hand that wrapped the thread, hold the point of the needle firmly. With the thumb and index finger of your other hand, tightly hold and pull this wrapped thread off the eye end of the needle and down the length of the thread. This should leave a knot in the end of the thread.

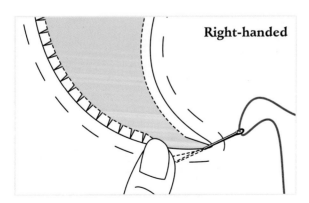

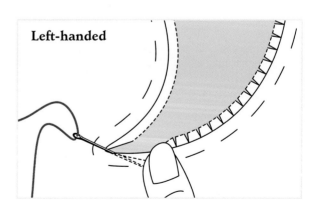

Slide the side of the needle along the marked line to turn the fabric under.

Thumb-press the turned edge in place when you see that the pencil mark will be hidden and the edge will be smooth. (Keep your thumb close to your stitching.) Move your thumb a little to the left with each stitch you take, revealing the spot you will sew next.

Insert the needle. From underneath the layers, insert the needle and bring it up, through all the layers, into an outside point. The needle should come out about two threads away from the point. Make all of the subsequent appliqué stitches from the top.

Start stitching. Begin sewing toward your thumb, which needs to hold down the edge ¼" to ½" away from the needle. Push the needle down into the bottom fabric, opposite the hole where the thread comes up. Run the needle point along the back of the project and bring it up again right at the turned edge, so the thread will be nearly hidden where it loops over the fold. (Use a stitch about ¹⁄₁₆" to ⅛" long.) This is called the hidden appliqué stitch or slipstitch.

Check the stitch length. You can check the length of your stitches by turning the project over. The stitches will show on the back, but they should not show on the front. Keep your stitches small, ⅛" or less. Continue stitching.

Reposition the fabric. When you can see that the pencil line is beginning to show, reposition the fabric in your left hand so that, when you needle-turn, you are always sliding your needle down from left to right, while turning the fabric under.

> **TIP.** I have found that it helps me immensely if I lean my hands on my knee or other stable place while turning the fabric under with the needle. The palm of my right hand helps hold the fabric taut, and I've even found this position helps to steady a shaky hand.

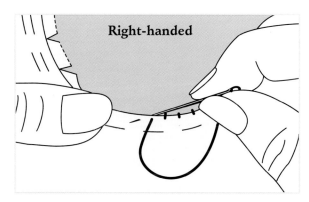

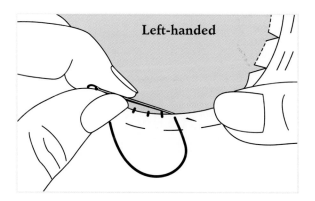

Appliqué stitch, also called slipstitch. Reposition the fabric and hold the allowance under with your thumb.

Outside points. On an outside point or right angle, take several tiny, close stitches at the point to secure the loose threads. Don't allow stray threads in the fabric to escape. Remember, you are the boss. Make them behave! Tuck a loose thread under and take a stitch over it to hold it there. After the shape is completely stitched, the loose threads and raw edges will be secure, and you need not worry about how little fabric was turned under.

Inside points. To make inside points sharper, stitch clear to the point on one side and secure the point with an extra tiny stitch. Turn the point under, straight across the tip then turn under the other side of the point until the pencil mark does not show. Using your thumb to hold the point securely, tug on the thread to make the point as sharp as you can then stitch down the other side of the point.

Enjoy your lacy reward. Continue cutting and sewing all of the shapes. I usually cut and sew the outside edge of the design last because it is my reward for finishing all the shapes.

TIPS

➤ When trying to turn under just a stray thread of the fabric, the point of the needle could make it fray further. Push the point of the needle under the fold and turn the fabric or stray thread under with the side of the needle.

➤ The tip of your needle could have a burr. If this is the case, the burr will catch and fray the edge of the fabric as it is being turned under. It's time to get a new needle.

➤ If there is too much fabric to turn under for a sharp point, you probably are using too wide an allowance. Keep allowances between 1/16" and 1/8".

➤ If there is a point that you want to look really sharp, extend your stitch a few threads straight out past the point.

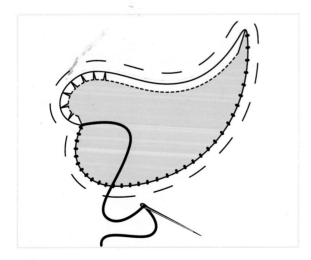

Turn the point under straight across the tip.

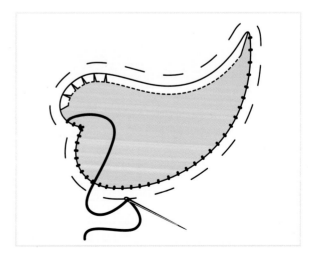

Continue turning the fabric under.

Adding a New Background

Trim excess bottom fabric. If the whole lacy piece will be appliquéd to a different block background, turn the piece over and, from the wrong side, cut away the excess bottom fabric ³⁄₁₆" from the stitching.

Baste and stitch. Choose a fabric that will be the background for the whole design (gold for the Heart of Rose block). Center the design on the background fabric and baste ¼" inside the outer edge of the design and around each shape to be appliquéd. Cut out, clip, and stitch the remaining negative shapes. The block background (gold) will show in these shapes.

Appliqué shapes. Cut the excess fabric away from the outer edge of the piece, leaving a ⅛" to ³⁄₁₆" turn-under allowance. Clip the inside curves and points in the outside edge and stitch the design to the background with the same slipstitch you used for the negative shapes. What a sense of accomplishment!

ABOVE: PURPLE PASSION VEST by Linda G. Howell, West Islip, New York. Add lacy appliqué to a garment pattern or a purchased vest or bag.

RIGHT: Heart of Rose block, front of block. The rose and leaf fabrics were appliquéd before the heart was basted to the gold background. (Pattern on author's Web site.)

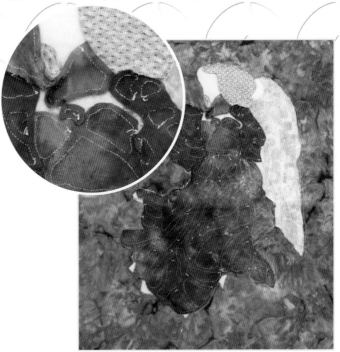

Front of Angel with Bird block (Pattern on author's Web site)

Back of Angel with Bird block. Fabric was trimmed from behind the angel to reduce bulk.

Cut away the background. If the whole design has been stitched onto a different background fabric, you may want to cut away the background fabric underneath the design to reduce bulk and to make quilting the layers easier.

Fixing Mistakes

Scissors slip. What if you cut the wrong space or outside the marked line? Relax. When stitching a lacy design, you can be sure that, if a shape is different from the pattern, it probably will not even be noticeable. If the design is symmetrical, you can cut and stitch the opposite side to match the one where your scissors slipped. You can rest assured that your block will be beautiful. It doesn't have to be exactly like the printed pattern.

Positive-image slip. If you make an unintentional cut in the positive image, just make another shape or extend an existing shape. You will be the only one who knows

that your piece doesn't match the pattern.

While stitching the outside edge of my Butterfly 2 pattern, I inadvertently cut through the base of the left antenna. What to do? I had only cut through it the width of my allowance, so I decided to begin the base of the antenna from the end of my cut and reshape it a little as I moved up the antenna. If I had not pointed it out to you, you probably would not be able to notice that the left antenna is a little out of place. If you can't tell, why should it matter?

Negative-image slip. Don't ever be afraid of sticking your scissors into the slash in a shape and trimming away fabric. So far, I've never cut into the background fabric while doing this step. However, if you should accidentally cut the background, it is the easiest thing to fix, and no one, but no one would ever know. (Except you, of course!) Follow the illustrations on page 33 to fix a negative-image slip.

FIXING MISTAKES

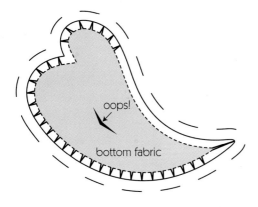

Scissors slip in the bottom fabric while cutting away the top fabric

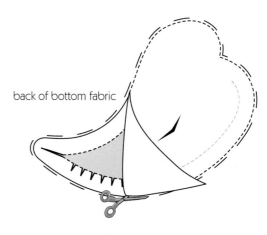

From the back, cut away the bottom fabric inside the basting stitches.

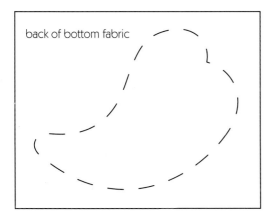

Match the grain of the fabric and baste a scrap of fabric over the cutout shape. Pin the scrap to the back; stitch from the front.

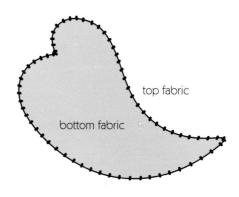

Appliqué the shape and remove the basting stitches.

Butterfly 2. Can you tell which antenna was cut? (Pattern on author's Web site.)

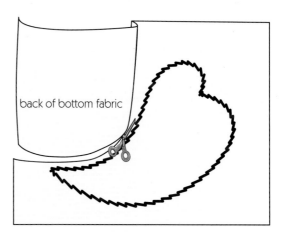

Turn the piece over and cut away the scrap, leaving a ³⁄₁₆" allowance around the shape.

Stuffed Work

When the appliqué is complete, you may want to use trapunto or cording to add dimension to your piece. "Trapunto" is another name for stuffed work. Soft cording or yarn can also be used to add a raised channel effect.

Add stuffing or cording after the block has been completed because both methods will leave imperfections on the back of your project. These will be hidden in the quilt when the batting and backing are added.

Trapunto or cording details may be needed in areas of the positive image that are wide and could use some extra detailing. If adding cording to a leaf design, sew your channels where the veins of the leaf would be.

FILLING WITH BATTING

With a quilting needle and thread to match the top fabric, add a running stitch in a shape that would be pleasing to stuff and become prominent within the positive image. This stitch resembles a closely spaced quilting stitch.

Make a small incision into the bottom fabric inside the stitched shape. Tear off a small amount of quilt batting and stuff it into the incision with a chopstick. (A surgical instrument called a hemostat would also work.) Be sure not to overstuff because it might cause puckering in the positive image.

After the shape has been stuffed to your satisfaction, stitch the incision closed with a couple of loose crisscrossed stitches to keep the stuffing in.

FILLING WITH YARN OR CORDING

For yarn or cording, use a thread to match the positive-image fabric and sew two parallel lines of running stitches, forming a channel. Keep your stitches neat and consistent.

After the channel is sewn, thread cotton yarn into a large darning needle and enter the channel from the back of the piece. Feed the needle through the channel without catching the top fabric. Bring the needle out through the back when you reach the end of the section you are filling. If the channel makes a sharp turn, pull the needle out through the back at the turn and begin again for the other leg of the turn.

On the back of the block, at the beginning of a channel, leave a 1" tail. When you reach the end of a section or when you begin again at a sharp turn, leave a 1" tail again. The beginning and ending tails will act as "draws" for each section. If your quilt or the yarn shrinks during laundering, you can pull on the tails to keep the corded sections from puckering.

If you make the channels wider than the thickness of the yarn in some places, feed two or three pieces of yarn, next to each other, to fill the channel. Don't thread more than about three yarns because they might not stay flat. If the area is wider than three yarns, use the trapunto technique instead of yarn.

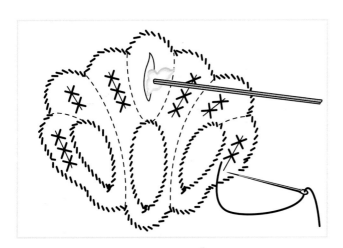

Stuffing a clamshell shape (back of block)

Summer Butterfly, 29½" x 24", by Dottie Perdue, Lancaster, Virginia. Stitch one block for a show-stopping wallhanging or combine several blocks for a throw.

"There is such a joyous reward working on these lacy appliqué designs. There's something very restorative in watching the shape emerge from the fabric."

Marilyn A. Bonomi, Hamden, Connecticut

Design with quilting stitches

Quilting Lacy Appliqué

Let the lacy design suggest a quilting design. Quilt closely around the appliquéd edge in the negative spaces to stitch them down and allow the positive image to pop out even more.

Quilt around the outside edge of the lacy design. You can add a second quilting line (echo) ¼" outside the first one. Then use filler quilting in the background around the design. Crosshatching or diagonal lines are good choices for this filler quilting.

Add quilting on the positive design only where details need to be added and stuffed work has not been used. A good example of this would be the Celtic Knots pattern (page 76). The woven look of the channels can be created by quilting over some of the channels.

Quilting lines create the illusion of weaving in the Celtic Knots block.

Beginning Pattern Design

After you have made one or several of the lacy appliqué patterns on pages 54–109, you may find that you would like to design a pattern of your own. Designing lacy appliqué is really easy and fun to do.

Supplies

You will need a few tools for drawing your pattern:

A sheet of paper a few inches larger than your desired design

6–8 sharp #2 pencils

Several good erasers

Curved drafting tools, stencils, or quilting templates

Template plastic

Scissors for cutting the plastic

Pictures of openwork designs for inspiration

The endless supply of quilting design templates, drafting tools, and stencils on the market will be invaluable for drawing curved shapes for your cutout designs. These commercial templates do not contain all the elements necessary for designing lacy appliqué, but they do make good starting places. Use them along with your own made-up design shapes transferred onto template plastic and cut out. Using plastic templates will make the motifs easier to repeat over and over in your designing process.

SNOWFLAKE PILLOW, 15" x 17", by Margaret Stack, Wicomico Church, Virginia. Any single motif can be used for a pillow.

Antique cutwork with black embroidery on white linen

Finding Inspiration

You may be surprised to find that lacy appliqué designs can be inspired by many different stitching techniques and other art forms. I've taken a sampling of different stitching techniques, including Baltimore Album blocks and pieces from other cultures, and designed a lacy appliqué block to represent most of them. Here are some examples of other forms of artistic expression for inspiration:

Cutwork embroidery. In the past, the term "cutwork" was used for a technique of linen and thread-work embroidery called "white work." This technique can give a simple, plain piece of linen an elegant and slightly lacy appearance. In white work, threads are sewn closely in a buttonhole stitch. The fabric is cut away from inside the stitches, leaving open areas. The more areas that are cut, the lacier the design appears. The white

Antique linen with whitework

Romanian hand-made doily by Nicoleta Cojocaru, Romania

embroidery stitches are also a part of the design. Some of the shapes touch and overlap each other, leaving the stitching to stand alone. Hand embroidery in the form of bars or "brides" is stitched in some pieces, which adds to the lacy appearance.

Lace doilies. In Romania, there is a form of lace making that incorporates techniques from crochet and macramé. The lace is thick and heavy, and it reminds me more of a mat than a doily. These lace forms can also be translated into lacy appliqué.

Scherenschnitte. There is an art form of cutting paper known as "scherenschnitte," which literally means "scissors-snips" in German. The colonists brought this lovely art to America. This creative outlet of cutting intricate pictures from colored paper and placing them on a white background, or vice versa,

DEER IN THE WOODS, 7" x 9", by Ellen Haberlein, Falls Church, Virginia. Scherenschnitte paper-cut design.

MOOSE IN THE CLEARING, 18" x 17", designed and stitched by author, with permission from Ellen Haberlein. Scherenschnitte represented in lacy appliqué (pattern on pages 56–57).

ROMANIAN FLOWER BASKET, 9½" x 10", by the author, pattern on pages 82–83

has been around for hundreds of years. These beautiful and intricate designs, when enlarged, make good choices for lacy appliqué.

The intricacy that can be achieved with a razor-edged tool in cutting the scherenschnitte designs needs to be simplified when translating the designs into fabric. Sharp points, spaces, and shapes need to have enough fabric for turning under the edges when appliquéing. The spaces in both the positive and negative areas should be at least ¼" for ease in appliquéing. You can simplify a design by taking out some of the intricate details.

Hawaiian appliqué. For the Hawaiian method, the quilter folds a bed-sized piece of fabric into eighths and cuts the design directly into the fabric, like cutting a paper snowflake.

HAWAIIAN QUILT, 36½" x 43", stitched by the author. This quilt was made in the traditional Hawaiian method.

Then comes the task of carefully laying the large piece on the background fabric, pinning it in place, basting it down, and using needle-turn appliqué for stitching it.

I tried this technique. The step of unfolding the fabric and laying it flat on the background after it had been intricately cut out proved to be no easy task! I found that the cutwork appliqué method makes it much easier. I use a paper pattern to trace the design on the fabric and make only a tiny slash into each section to be cut out before pinning and basting the fabric to the background. I then cut the design as the piece is being appliquéd.

Pa Ndau appliqué. The most impressive work in the cutwork appliqué field is done by the Hmong people from Laos, Vietnam, and Thailand. Pa Ndau is a word that encompasses an entire needlework tradition, and it is passed from generation to generation among the Hmong.

The Pa Ndau or "cloth flowers" are symmetrical patterns worked on two to four layers of fabric. These stitched designs are used on items such as hats, purses, and aprons. You will find vendors selling these small intricate designs at our American quilt shows. It takes a very experienced cutwork appliquér to achieve this kind of work. If you have ever tried needle-turn appliqué, in any form, you will respect the work of the Hmong in a new way.

Finding more ideas. If you look at the world around you, you will be surprised at how often you see lacy openwork on all forms of decoration. One of the first things that comes to mind is a Victorian house with decorative porch rails and gingerbread designs

GLORY GARDEN, 8" x 8", stitched by Ia Moua Yang, Warren, Michigan. Red and yellow are traditional colors for Pa Ndau stitchery.

Architectural inspiration

ABOVE AND RIGHT: PALM LEAVES AND LACE FRAME, 32" x 48", stitched by the author

RIGHT: Victorian greeting card from which author designed PALM LEAVES AND LACE FRAME

Appliqué *Lace* Patterns ❧ Linda Pool

Think
of me

Victorian greeting card

ABOVE AND RIGHT: Metal and wood inspiration: candlestick, perfume bottle, and wood frame

in the upper corners of the porch overhangs and in the gables. This decorative work is usually cut from wood or made from wrought iron. These designs can be interpreted in cutwork on fabric as well. Imagine using these gingerbread designs in the corners of a quilt.

Victorian and other note cards cut by a press, or the newer versions cut by a laser, are great designs for translating into fabric. Some would need to be simplified for your sewing project.

Ceramic and wood cutouts can be used for inspiration and will provide many ideas. Fretwork, of all kinds, contains a wonderful storehouse of ideas. Metal trivets, jewelry, wrought-iron garden chairs, Victorian heater grills, lattice, ornate metal or wood picture frames, wallpaper borders, embossed wallpaper, decorative ceiling ornamentation, fancy printing designs, etc., are all great sources of inspiration.

PERMISSION FOR DESIGN USE

If you are designing a pattern and have used a tangible item for inspiration (in any medium: drawing, photography, sculpture, wood carving, metalwork, matchbook cover, etc.), please remember the copyright.

❧ Assume everything is copyrighted until you know otherwise.

❧ Don't hesitate to ask permission from the artist. Most will be happy to give it. Get all permissions in writing. Remember, if the artist says "No," no means no.

❧ With a few exceptions, material older than 75 years is in the public domain and therefore available for use.

❧ If you have taken your design from another source, no matter how much you manipulate it, you still need to get permission.

❧ Artwork, such as sculptures, on public property could be protected by copyright.

❧ When photographing private property, you need permission from the owner.

NOT A TABLECLOTH, 52" x 66", by Barbara K. Powers, Centreville, Virginia

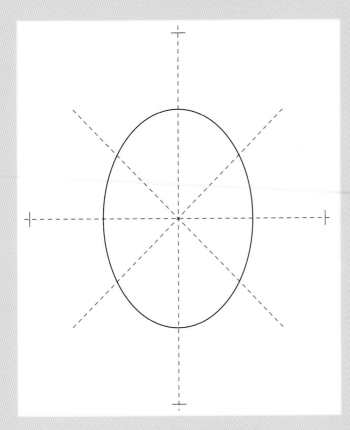

Oval with marked guidelines and outside edges

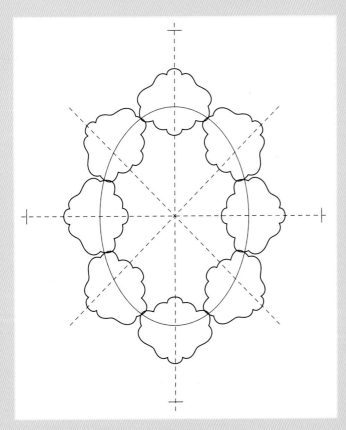

Placing motifs on the guidelines

Drawing a Design

The following instructions show how to create a lacy oval frame in a positive-image design. Once you understand how to draw this simple piece, you can use these same steps to make your own designs, starting with any basic shape, such as a circle, square, diamond, or heart.

Draw an oval. It should be approximately in the center of the sheet of paper. This oval will provide the basic structure for the frame design, so it should be large enough to contain any pattern you want to stitch in the center of the frame.

Mark guidelines. You will need the following guidelines for adding motifs around the oval frame: Fold the paper so the oval is divided in half horizontally, vertically, and diagonally. If you prefer, you can draw faint lines dividing the oval into equal sections.

Mark the outside edge. Decide the placement of the outside edge of the frame and mark it on all four sides of the paper, then work within this space while designing. You won't know exactly what the finished design will look like at this time, so allow a little extra space for changes and additions.

Draw a motif on template plastic. (Several possible motifs are given on page 109, or you can use one of your own design.) Cut the template. Place the template on the oval, centered on a vertical or horizontal guideline, and lightly trace around the template with a pencil. Repeat for each horizontal and vertical guideline. Then center additional motifs between those already drawn. Erase the original oval line as you go.

Add more motifs. Around the outside of the design, trace new motifs. Add as many as needed to fill the space. These are only beginning design lines at this time, and they create an interesting overall shape.

Connect motifs with bridges. Drawn shapes are positive images, so if there are gaps between the shapes in your design, they need to be connected by bridges over the negative space to give a lacy effect. These bridges take the place of the crocheted or twisted connecting threads found in real lace. Leave at least a ¼" wide bridge between shapes.

Add latticework. Draw parallel lines in the negative spaces at a 45-degree angle. Space the lines, alternating them between ¼" and ¾" apart. Draw the same lines in the opposite direction but do not draw over the previously drawn ¼" wide channels. This detailing needs to be done in only a quarter of the pattern because the quarter pattern can be rotated and traced to form the whole design. Latticework like this can be added to any design.

Make sure to draw a dashed line (shown in red) to define both sides of your quarter pattern. These lines will help you match the quarters for tracing. Do not draw this dashed line on your fabric.

Continue to erase. Always erase any lines that are unnecessary to your design. You will then be able to distinguish the positive and negative spaces much more easily.

Add negative shapes. When you draw negative shapes in a positive space, it adds a lot of interest to your design and gives it a lacier look. As you look at the whole design, the positive part should be ¼" to ¾" or wider in most areas. If it becomes too wide, however,

Motifs added to the design

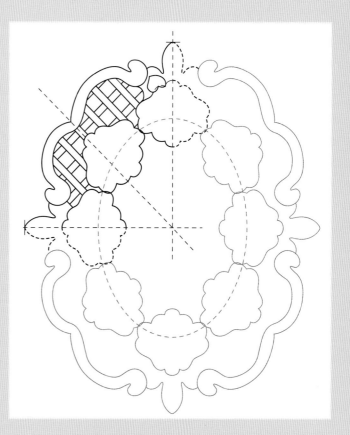

Adding lattice

Erase unnecessary lines.

detailing may need to be added in the form of stuffing (see Stuffed Work, page 34). Notice how using different negative shapes changes the look of the design.

The two designs are similar but different. Either version 1 or 2 would be wonderful to appliqué. There is no right way or wrong way, just what is pleasing to the eye.

"You started me on a reverse appliqué passion. Thank you for being my inspiration for a love of this technique."

Marilyn Nolte, Weems, Virginia

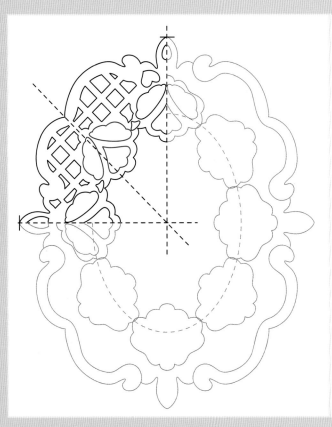

Negative shapes added, version 1

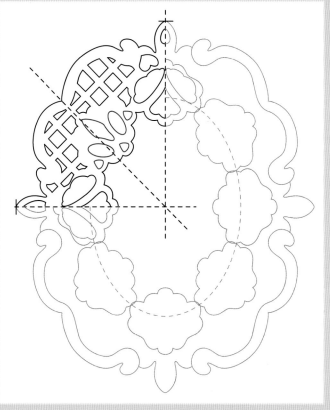

Version 2

Completed frame, version 1   Version 2

Darken the pattern for tracing. Because you have been drawing with a pencil, your marked pattern will not be dark enough to trace onto fabric. When you are satisfied with the design you have drawn, use a fine or extra-fine permanent black marker to trace over the lines of a quarter of your design. (If you like, you can retrace the quarter pattern on a clean sheet of paper.) Turn the paper over and retrace the lines on the back. Having the pattern on both sides of the paper will make it easier to flip and rotate the tracing as needed to draw the whole design on your fabric.

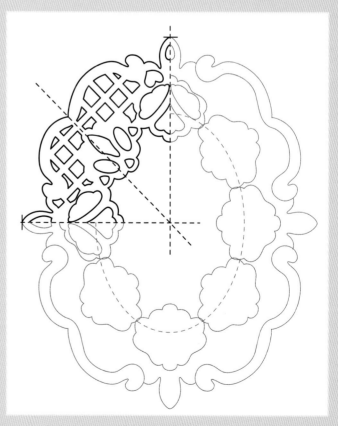

Darkened quarter of the design

TIPS. For a lacy look, many shapes need to be cut out of the positive fabric, allowing the bottom fabric to show through.

Pattern with too few shapes

Pattern with a good number of shapes

Make sure that your positive shapes are at least ¼" wide at the narrowest point to allow for covering the turn-under allowances. The negative spaces can be as small as ⅛" and still be needle-turned. However, don't put too many of these into your design because they can be tedious.

Squares are easy to reverse appliqué, and the more you put into your design, the lacier it looks.

Shapes with narrow pointed ends can be appliquéd, but the angle of the point should not be less than about 30 degrees. With a narrower angle, there will not be enough fabric to turn under.

HEART OF LOVE #4, 12" x 12½", designed and stitched by the author. This block contains many ¼" wide channels.

Points need to be 30 degrees or wider.

BALTIMORE ALBUM IN PURPLE, 88" x 103", by Maryiln Nolte, Weems, Virginia

Lacy Patterns

Lacy appliqué is suitable for many quilting, garment, and home decorating projects. Patterns can be animals, architectural, border designs, celtic designs, florals, frames, hearts, music inspired, snowflakes, or any design subject you wish to adapt to lace.

Enlarging and Reducing Patterns

The patterns can be used at the size given, or they can be enlarged or reduced as desired to fit your projects. Using a proportional scale will make it easy to find the percentage of enlargement. If you don't have a proportional scale, decide what block size would work for the pattern in the book, leaving the amount of space between the pattern and the block's edges that pleases you. Divide the block size you want by the original block size.

For example, Calico Cat by Any Other Name (page 58) would fit nicely in a 12" block. To enlarge the pattern to fit in an 18" block, divide 18" by 12", which equals 1.5. Multiply 1.5 by 100 to find the percent of enlargement, which is 150 percent. For a 24" block, 24" divided by 12" equals 2, times 100 equals 200 percent.

You can also reduce patterns, and lacy appliqué can be done successfully with rather small cutout shapes. For example, the Double Lace Frame pattern (page 86) is 14" x 16½", which would look good in a 22" x 24" block. It would be just as lovely at 80 percent of its present size for an overall dimension of about 11¼" x 13¼", which could be placed in a 19" x 21" block. On the other hand, it could be enlarged 150% to measure 21" x 24¾" and be used in a 31" x 35" wallhanging.

*Reverse right half of heart
to make left half.*

top

bottom

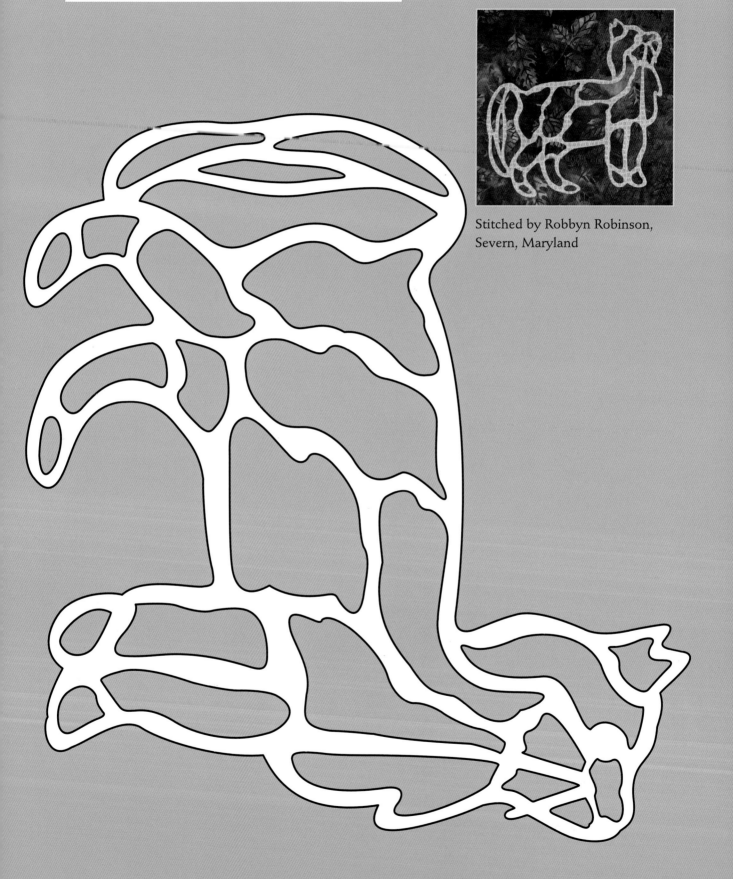

Stitched by Robbyn Robinson,
Severn, Maryland

LACE AND FLORAL BUTTERFLY WITH EYELET EDGING BORDER,
36" x 29", by the author. Pattern on pages 60–63.

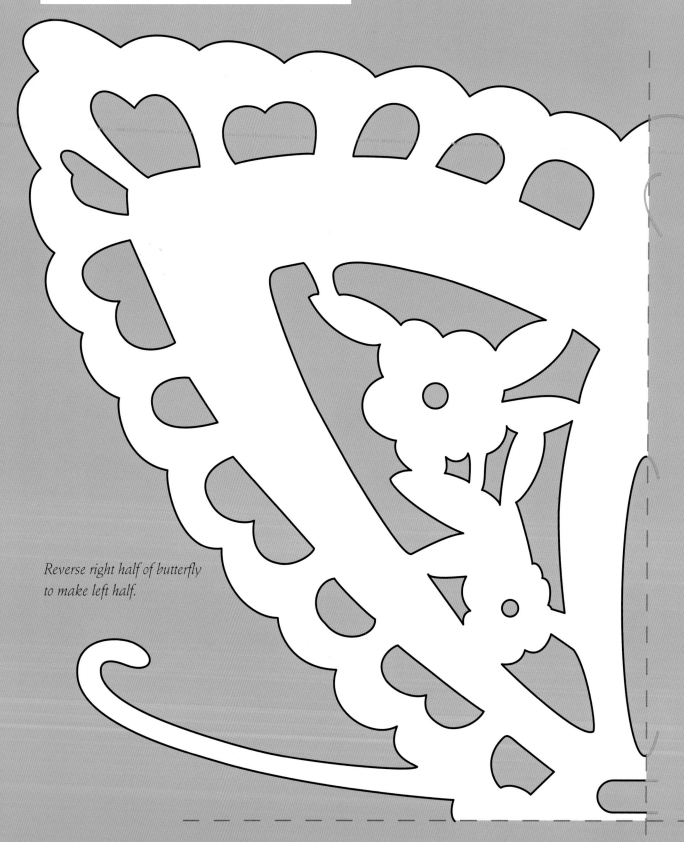

Reverse right half of butterfly to make left half.

top   bottom

Rotate pattern to make the other three corners.

corner

side

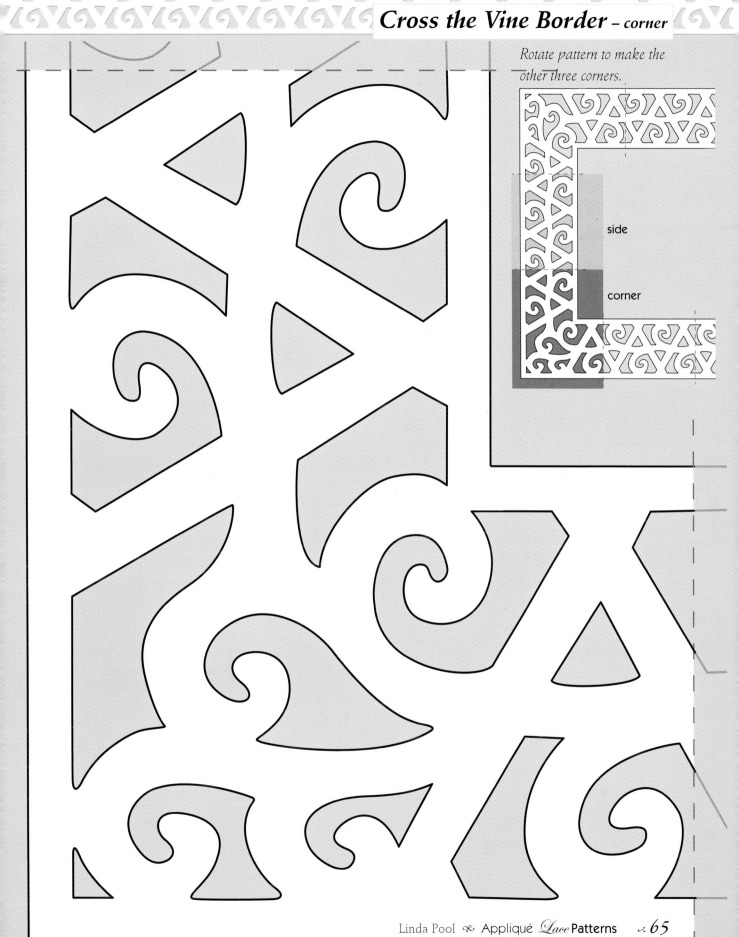

Rotate pattern to make the other three corners.

side

corner

Open-Worked Border – side

Open-Worked Border – corner

side

corner

*Rotate pattern to make the
other three corners.*

Lacy Border

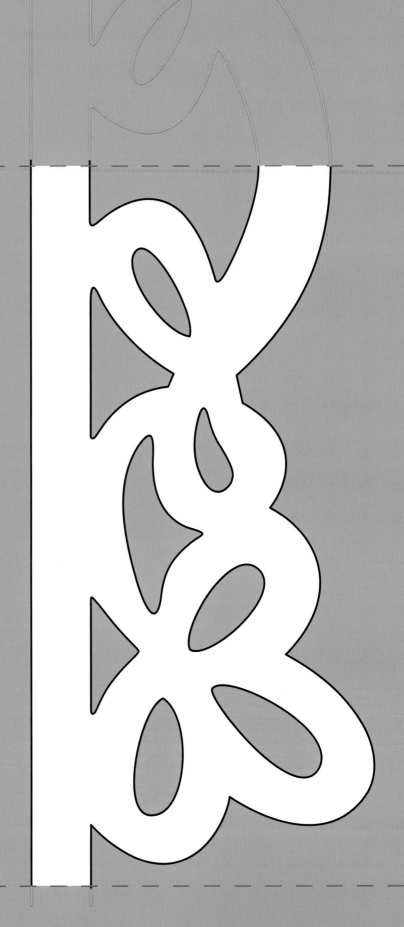

Appliqué *Lace* Patterns ❧ Linda Pool

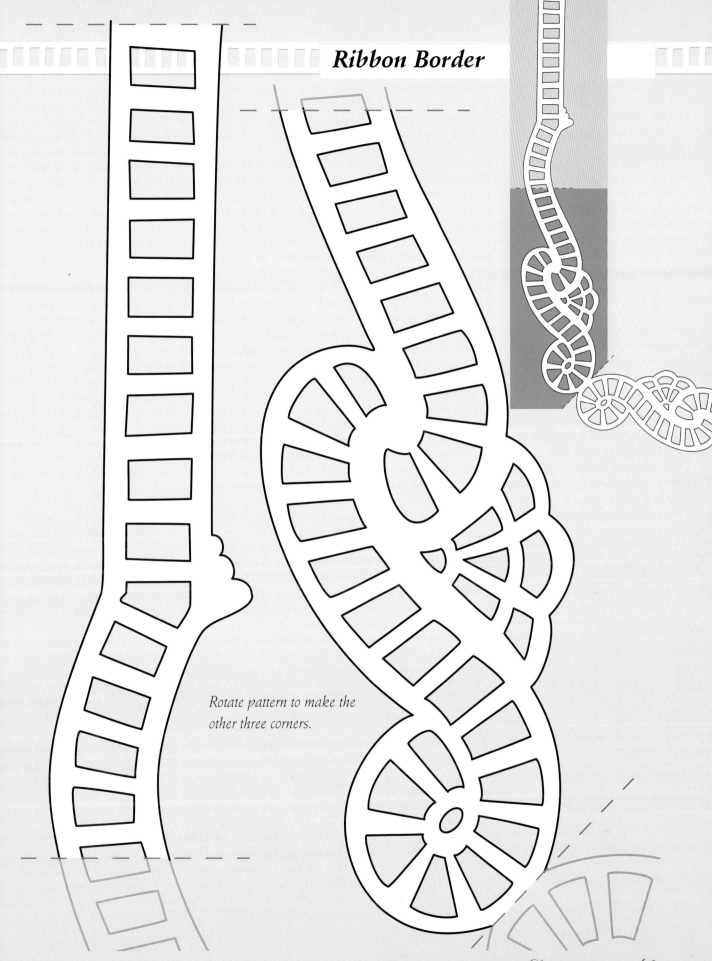

Ribbon Border

Rotate pattern to make the other three corners.

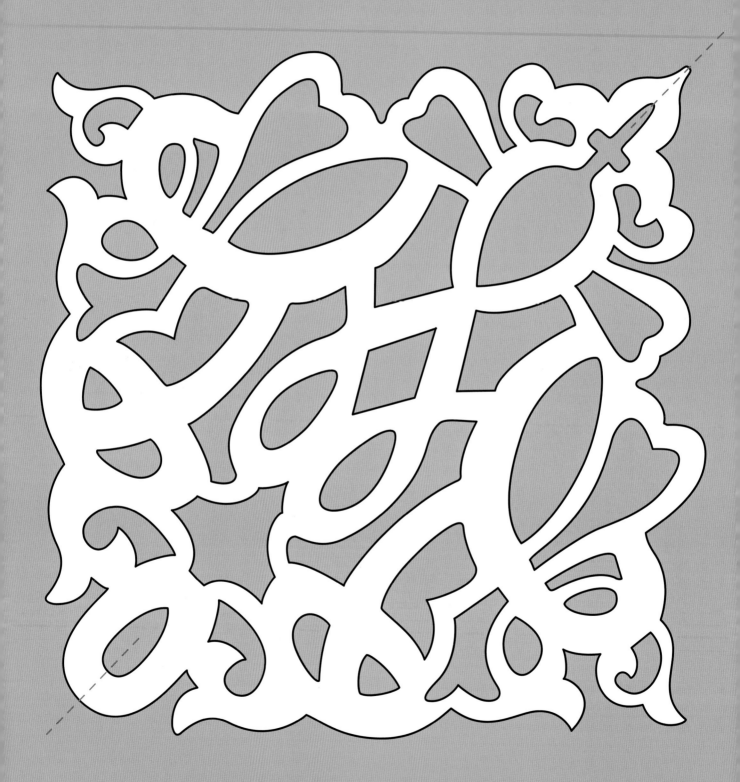

GAZEBO, 7½" x 7¾", by the author

Quilt Top Decoration

*Reverse pattern to make the
other half of design.*

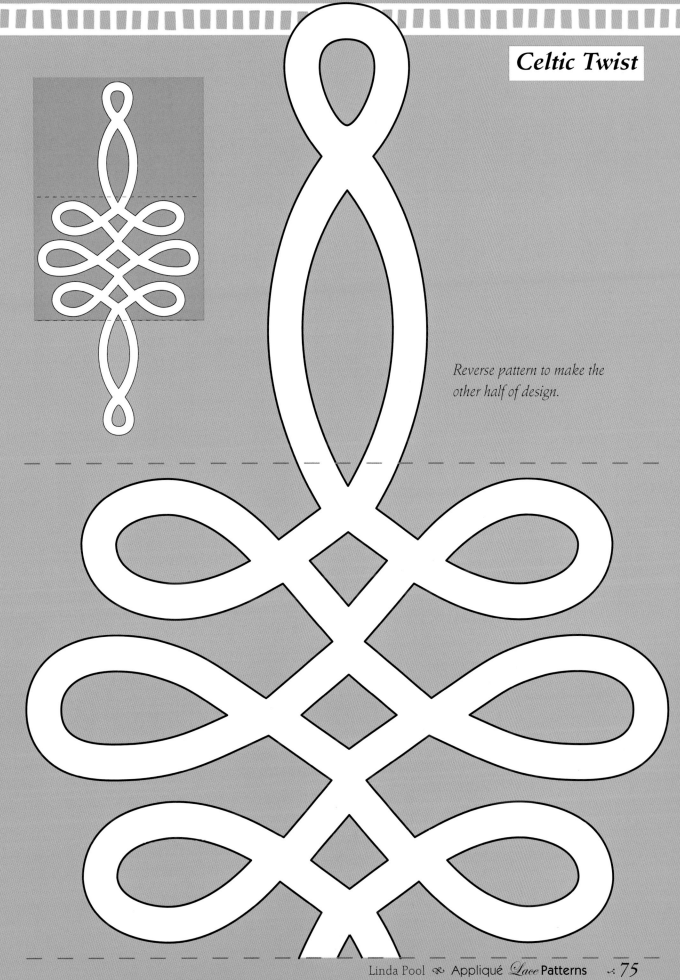

Celtic Twist

*Reverse pattern to make the
other half of design.*

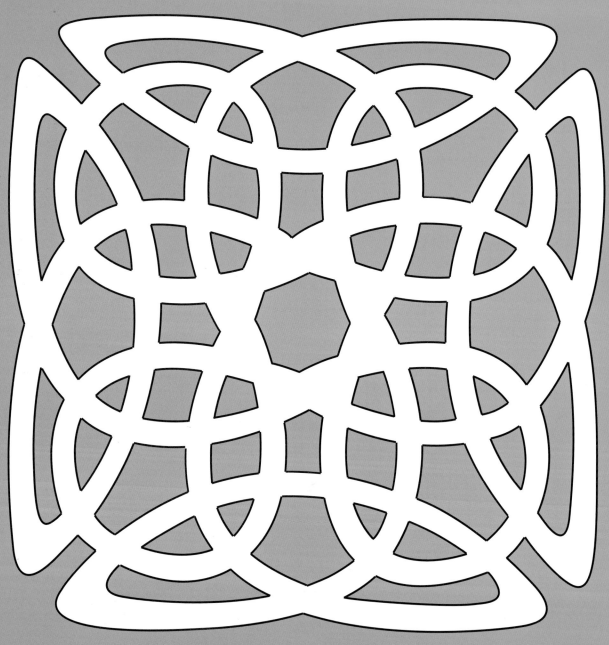

LACY FLOWER BASKET, 17" x 15", by the author. Pattern on pages 78–79.

top right

bottom right

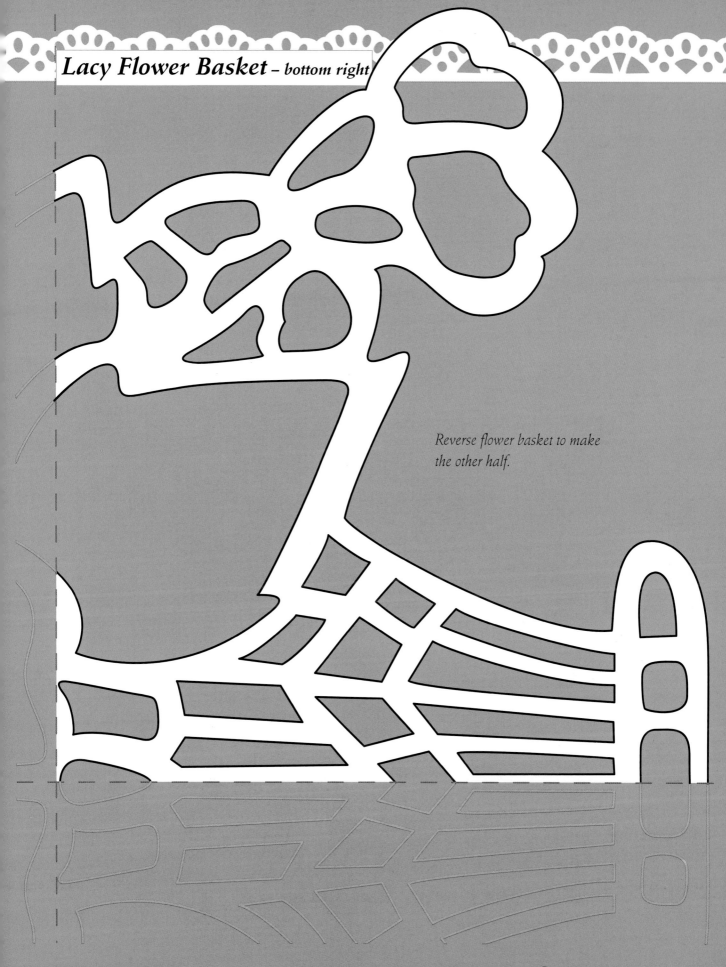

Lacy Flower Basket – *bottom right*

Reverse flower basket to make the other half.

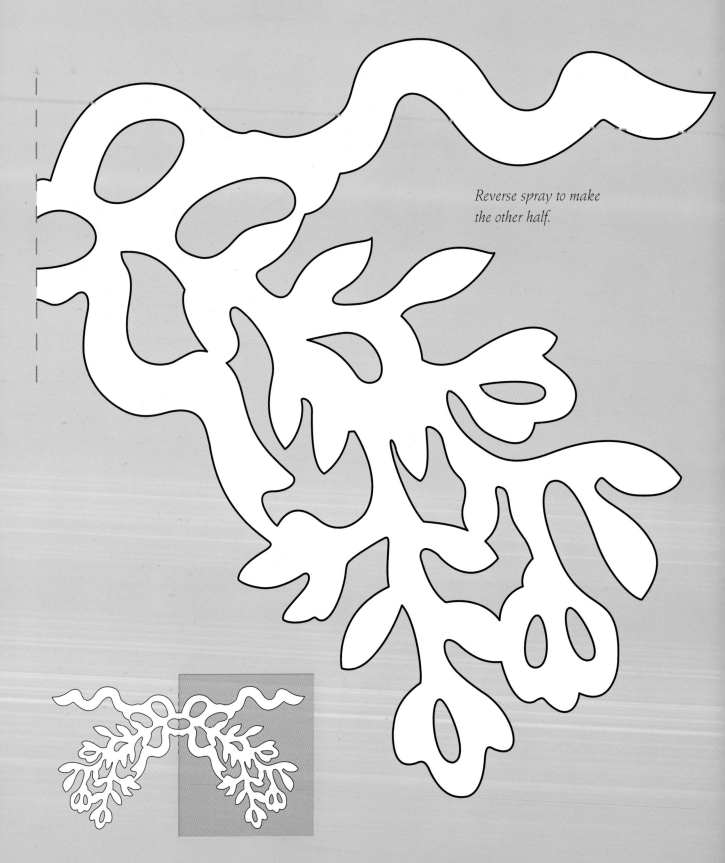

Reverse spray to make the other half.

ROMANIAN FLOWER BASKET, 9½" x 10", by the author. Pattern on pages 82–83.

left   right

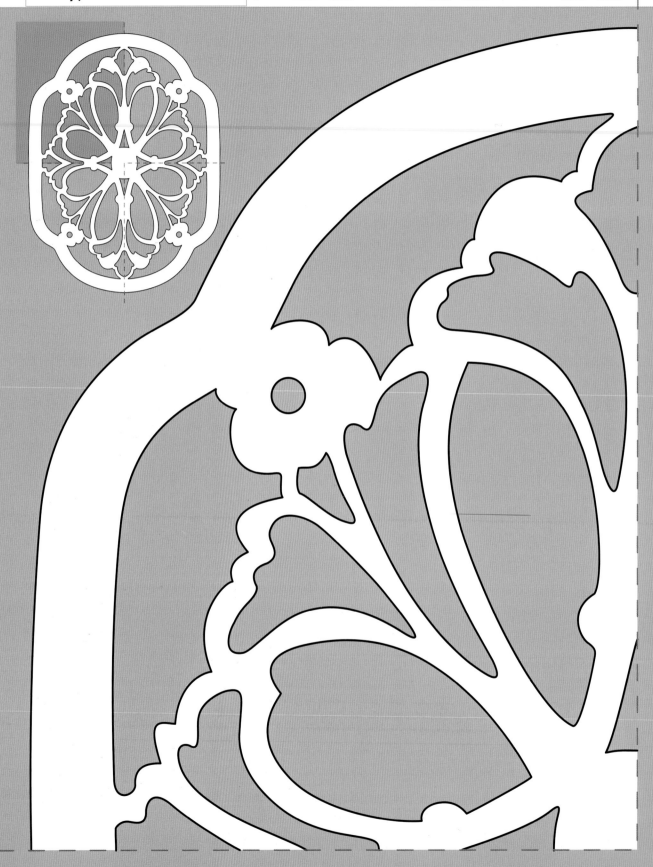

Double Lace Frame

Frame design courtesy of Lenox, Incorporated,
Lawrenceville, New Jersey

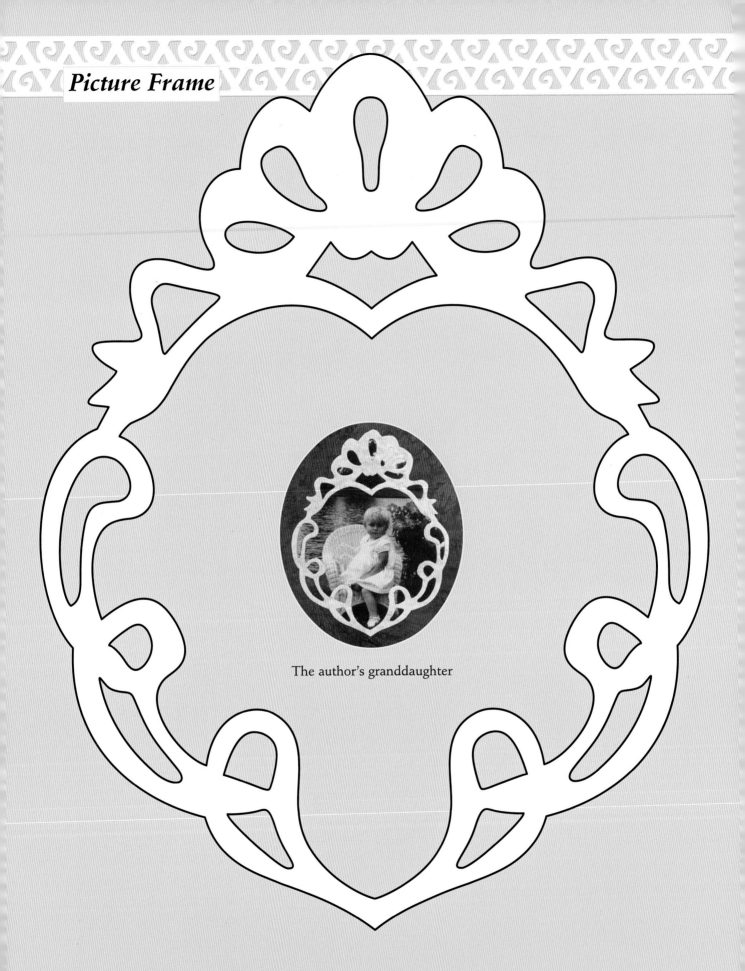

The author's granddaughter

Love Birds

Stitched by Sara Madson, Crowley, Texas

Linda Pool ❧ Appliqué *Lace* Patterns ∴ 89

Stained Glass Bow

STAINED GLASS BOW, 7½" x 8⅜", stitched by Fran Snay, Burleson, Texas

Lyre

Fancy Music

Stitched by Barbara K. Powers, Centreville, Virginia

Antique Book
Embossing –top

*Reverse right half of design
to make left half.*

top

bottom

Antique Book Embossing –bottom

3-D Illusion

Design courtesy of Lenox, Incorporated,
Lawrenceville, New Jersey

Paper-Cut Snowflake

LEFT: PAPER-CUT SNOWFLAKE, 17" x 14¾", stitched by Anita Askias, Annapolis, Maryland

Tin Snowflake

RIGHT: TIN SNOWFLAKE, 17¾" x 20½", stitched by Stephanie Pool, Studio City, California

Angel Snowflake

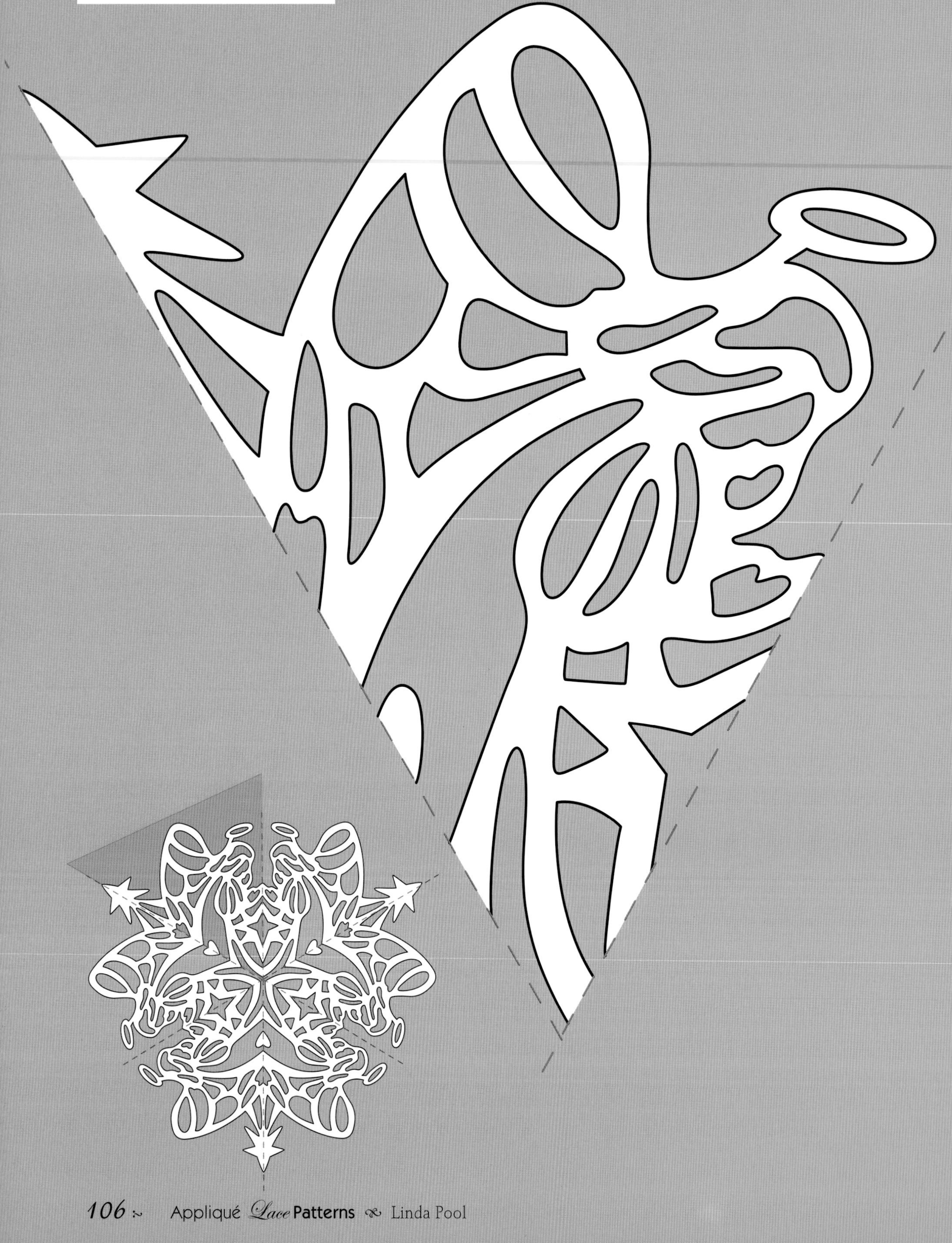

Crèche

Stitched by Barb Celio, Vienna, Virginia

Appliqué *Lace* Patterns ✥ Linda Pool

Bibliography

Eaton, Jan. *Letts Creative Needlecraft: Embroidering Table Linen*. London: Charles Letts & Company Ltd., 1990.

Ganderton, Lucinda. *The Potter Needlework Library: Appliqué*. New York: Clarkson Potter/Publishers, 1996.

Lawther, Gail. *Celtic Quilting*. Devon: David & Charles, 1998.

Marshall, Suzanne. *Take-Away Appliqué*. Paducah, KY: American Quilter's Society, 1998.

Mathews, Kate. *MOLAS!: Patterns, Techniques & Projects for Colorful Appliqué*. Ashville, NC: Lark Books, 1998.

Morris, William & Marty Noble, ed. *William Morris Iron-On Transfer Patterns*. New York: Dover Publications, Inc., 2003.

Pahl, Ellen, ed. *The Quilters Ultimate Visual Guide*. Emmaus, PA: Rodale Press, Inc., 1997.

Root, Elizabeth. *Hawaiian Quilting*. New York: Dover Publications, Inc., 1989.

Sienkiewicz, Elly. *Baltimore Beauties and Beyond*. Lafayette, CA: C & T Publishing, 1989.

Seward, Linda. *The Complete Book of Patchwork, Quilting and Appliqué*. Mineola, New York, NY: Prentice Hall Press, 1987.

Strombeck, Janet A. & Richard H. *Gazebos and Other Garden Structure Designs*. New York: Sterling Publishing Co., Inc., 1983.

Yang, Ia Moua. *Pa Ndau, The Textile Art of the Hmong*. Warren, MI.

Meet the Author

Linda Pool is known for several distinctive quilts: THE BRIDE, which won five viewer's choice awards in a row at major shows; THE GREATEST MOMENTS OF A GIRL'S LIFE, documented in Quilters' S.O.S – Save our Stories, by The Alliance for American Quilts; and LINDA'S LACE, which was nominated as "One of the Best Quilts of the Twentieth Century." She is a three-time winner in the Great American Quilt Contest sponsored by The Museum of American Folk Art in New York City. She has won various other awards and ribbons in major shows, and her quilts have been shown in numerous quilt shows and magazines around the world.

She has been quilting since 1977 and has taught classes and lectured about quilting techniques since 1982. Linda was a member of the Jinny Beyer Hilton Head Island Quilting Seminar staff for ten years and has taught at other major quilt shows, retreats, and seminars. She is a regular as a needlework show judge as well as having judged many quilt shows.

She loves to share her knowledge of quiltmaking with anyone expressing an interest. She has been known to send her lacy appliqué patterns to flight hostesses, kiosk vendors, young mothers looking for a relaxing project, and young women who commented on a project she was stitching. She wants to spread the word and have people everywhere enjoy lacy appliqué.

Linda lives in Vienna, Virginia, with her husband, Don. They have four grown children. In addition to making quilts and creative Christmas decorations, Linda is the bookkeeper for the family car repair business. She enjoys reading, singing, and painting, when there is time.

Currently, Linda is the owner of Very Victorian, LLC, which is a pattern company with a line of lacy appliqué patterns for quilters. You can find these patterns on her Web site: www.lindaslace.com.

other AQS Books

This is only a small selection of the books available from the American Quilter's Society. AQS books are known worldwide for timely topics, clear writing, beautiful color photos, and accurate illustrations and patterns. The following books are available from your local bookseller, quilt shop, or public library.

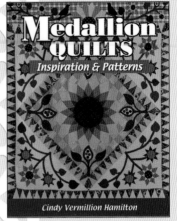

#6905   us$24.95

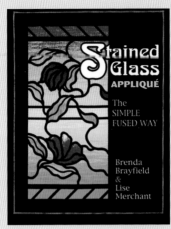

#6671   us$21.95

#6804   us$22.95

#6903   us$19.95

#6899   us$21.95

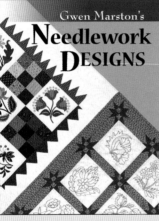

#6896   us$22.95

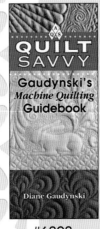

#6898

#6519

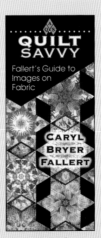

#6413

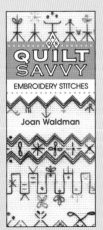

#6520

Quilt Savvy Series

4¼" x 10⅞"

us$21.95 each

Look for these books nationally.
Call or **Visit** our Web site at

1-800-626-5420
www.AmericanQuilter.com